The Magic Peasant

HENRY BREWIS

Farming Press
Wharfedale Road, Ipswich, UK.

First published 1986

ISBN 0 85236 162 9

British Library Cataloguing in Publication Data

Brewis, Henry
   The magic peasant.
   1. Agriculture——Anecdotes, facetiae,
   satire, etc.
   I. Title
   630'.2'017   S521
   ISBN 0-85236-162-9

Typeset by Galleon Photosetting, Ipswich
Printed and bound in Great Britain by
Redwood Burn Ltd, Trowbridge

Foreword

This does not pretend to be a deep, meaningful book; it doesn't concern itself with a host of smouldering issues, the kind that might inflame hairy young academics on the left, or balding superannuated aristocrats on the right, or even deviant index-linked townies in the middle. Social problems such as inner city deprivation, teenage glue sniffing, the threat of nuclear war, and the inevitability of Terry Wogan on our television screens, may well demand serious consideration somewhere, – but this is not the place. If anything, this is designed to be a brief refuge from all that stuff.

It is essentially a rural book, an everyday story, in pictures and verse, of peasant folk, – and in particular a fellow called Sep.

My dictionary describes a peasant as a 'small farmer, a tiller of soil, a countryman'. It implies he might be a bit rough, unrefined, even awkward and stubborn, – and that sounds fair to me. But Sep is possibly a wee bit more than just an obstinate old country character, he might almost represent a peculiar rural philosophy as well, – and if that sounds a touch pompous, well, so be it, – I think it's right enough. Certainly anybody, man or woman, who can survive the slings and arrows of outrageous agriculture, especially in this climate, for nigh on a lifetime, and remain more or less sane, has got to be some sort of philosopher, even a magician, – and preferably one with a convenient memory, that pulls triumphs out of a hatful of disasters.

Well, how else could we endure the traumatic lambing in which yowes conspire to destroy us physically and mentally one spring, and still instruct the tup to arrange another pantomime for next year, and the next, and the next? How else could we come to terms with a beautiful, potentially profitable crop of corn being eaten by slugs while we slept, or flattened by a thunderstorm just as we got the combine out of the shed? Those who aren't properly equipped to cope with the normal farming disasters that fall from an uncertain sky every week are liable to go bananas.

So I reckon it does take a special sort of character to be a peasant, – even if the philosophy is very fundamental, and the magic more like luck.

Sep then is hardly the 'Panorama' farmer townie viewers generally see, articulating easily on grain surpluses and EEC inadequacies, while leaning nonchalantly on his shooting stick or his Range Rover. While that's going on our Sep will be at the mart, protesting to a coven of wholesale butchers that his bullocks are losing a bloody fortune, or back home cursing his VAT return, or trying to bale a field of hay before it rains, or 'setting on' a spare lamb to a reluctant yow, or feeding silage to ravenous cows, – or just complaining to his wife, his dog, anybody, anything within earshot, that the gods are agin him again.

They often are of course, but if he couldn't laugh at them now and then, he couldn't be a peasant.

'. . . right, then, now the little brats are away t' bed, – who's for some party games . . .?'

'. . . there y' are, then, pet, I bet that's the best snowman for miles around here . . .'

'. . . oh no, y' didn't wish him a Happy New Year, did y' . . .?'

'. . . I spy with my little eye, something beginning with . . .'

'. . . it's the same every time he's had a night on the beer, – next morning we never get fed properly . . .'

Any Fool Can Be a Farmer

'Any fool can be a farmer
in fact it helps no end
to be a little crazy
and half-way round the bend
it's not essential to be crackers
good gracious not at all
but it's no good being normal
while you're climbing up the wall . . .
if you can't meet these requirements
no need to break your heart
'cos you'll quickly get the hang of things
once you get a start
if the weather doesn't beat you
it'll be an awkward yow
or a brainless politician
or an old demented cow
or a collie dog that's useless
one that drives you quite insane
but you'll get there if you're lucky
and you'll hardly feel the pain
you'll have diseases in your barley
and pigeons on your wheat
temperamental old machinery
and a labrador in heat . . .

but by now you'll be conditioned
you'll accept that you're just mad
and you'll never swop the townie
for his posh suburban pad
let him keep his indexed pension
and his room without a view
but be sure to marry someone
who is crazy just like you. . . .'

'. . . I bought it for 'er Christmas present, – she was very impressed at the time . . .'

'. . . we could be in trouble, girls, the man's a nervous wreck, you'd think he'd never done a lambin' in his life before . . .'

'. . . with a temper like yours, sheep could well become another endangered species . . .'

'. . . Mother, do I *have* t' be a farmer when I grow up . . .?'

Animal 'Magic'

'He's late this morning,' said the four-crop mule as she limped nearer the troughs, with her big fat belly trailing close to the ground. 'I'm famished and the hay hecks are empty. . . .'

Her companion grinned, showing her one remaining wobbly tooth. 'Maybe he's had some trouble with the hoggs,' she suggested, 'y' know what wild, brainless creatures they can be, – perhaps one of them lambed and he can't catch her. I know if I could still run that fast I'd be off as well, but m' feet are killing me these days. . . .'

'I hear a gimmer died last night,' said the big-bellied yow, '. . . just a gimmer, y' know, in the full bloom of youth, and perfectly alright yesterday.'

'Pretty sudden wasn't it?' said wobbly tooth.

'Well, not really, – she was always a hell of a moody bitch, she would just stop eating for no reason at all, – and if that dog Sweep ever had a go at her, she'd stand away by herself for a whole day with her head down, slavering and threatening to collapse in a huff.'

'Yes, I suppose she was pretty good at that sort of thing.'

'Talking of Sweep, – I think he's slowing down quite a bit these days, don't you? – he's definitely taking short cuts, – I'm sure if you don't want to be gathered in, all you have to do is wander off from the rest of the girls, – and he'll ignore you. He doesn't like going out wide if he can help it. He can still be fairly nasty in-bye, of course, and if old Sep starts shouting at 'im he'll have your back leg or your top lip as quick as a flash.'

'That's right enough,' said wobbly tooth, – 'but what can y' expect with that foul-mouthed bloke screaming abuse? The dog feels he's got to do something dramatic, so he takes a lump out of one of us . . . and then Sep swears at him for biting, and throws his stick at 'im. Poor dog doesn't know what to do. Of course I can remember when Sweep was almost a trial dog. When he first came here (I was just a hogg m'self then), – what an eye he had, you couldn't beat him, stamp your foot as much as y' like, but the little black sod wouldn't let you past, – you had t' respect him. . . .'

'Here he is now,' said big belly, 'peeing on that thistle over there. Funny things, dogs, aren't they? – anyway Sep can't be far behind with the feed. I do like that new batch of high protein nuts, delicious, they're great, I'm goin' to stuff m'self this morning.'

'Be careful, now, remember what happened to that greedy two-crop Suffolk, – fat as lard, she was, and every morning she just put her bottom jaw into the trough and shovelled up the feed. She couldn't swallow it quick enough, pushed us all out of the way, like a bloody tank with a fore-end loader. She choked t' death last week y' know.'

'Never!'

'She did! Sep was foaming, – he hadn't got the troughs turned over before she was coughing and spluttering her last. You could tell he was upset, – he kicked her and punched her and smashed his stick, called her some terrible names. She'd been a gonna for quarter of an hour before he realised it was hopeless, he was positively deranged for a while. We all went away and kept very quiet until he was finished.'

'Oh he can be dangerous, that's for sure,' said fat belly. 'I remember when I had that big stupid single lamb last year, he tried to persuade me to take on somebody else's snivelling little triplet as well. I insisted it had nothing to do with me, I told him I was not responsible for other people's cast-off brats, – but old Sep shut me in a pen for days on end, beat the living daylights out of me, made m' nose bleed, – and stuffed this rubbishy crit

in for a suck four times a day. In the end I sat on the little bugger, and that was the end of that!'

'You did well, dear, – I mean, looking after your own is bad enough, I always say, and for another thing, with those orphans you can never know who the father was. Could be anybody, – those tups are all the same, wham bang and goodbye in late October, then you never see them again for a year, – I shudder to think what they get up to in the meantime.'

'Not a lot, I suspect, – they look absolutely knackered by mid-November.'

'Thats's true,' agreed wobbly tooth.

'So how many lambs are you going to have this time?'

'Well, I think I'll have twins, – Sep seems to like twins, – he gives you extra trough feed for a bit longer, and sometimes even puts you onto the maiden seeds field, and that's fantastic.'

'Actually I feel I could lamb today,' said big belly, – 'in fact as soon as we're fed I think I'll wander off to the far corner and look for a quiet spot to get started. I'll probably wait till after dark, though, otherwise that crazy half-bred bitch is sure to poke her nose in – she's tried to pinch every lamb that's been born so far, – and I wouldn't be surprised if she's geld. Sep clouts her every time but it has no effect, – it doesn't seem to hurt. . . .'

'Well, when you eventually get round to lambing, for God's sake do it yourself, – wait until Sep's having his supper or a kip, – if he has to do his midwifery trick you could be in trouble.'

'What do you mean . . . ?' asked big belly.

'Well, haven't you seen his hands? – they're enormous, and what's more when he's finished he'll inject you with everything he's got, – he carries a whole chemist's shop in his coat pockets these days, y' know, – I think he could be a drug addict. Anyway, here comes the tractor now, – what's he got in the link box today?'

'Two bales of hay and a bag of ewe nuts as usual,' said big belly eagerly, – 'and that dead gimmer I was telling you about. . . .'

'Never mind her, she's had it, – let's get to the troughs or there'll be nothing left, – careful, though, for God's sake don't knock the old fool down in the clarts, or he'll go stark raving mad again. . . .'

'. . . wasn't me, Gladys, – never sent a Valentine in m' life . . .'

'. . . and I get the impression the lambin's not goin' too well either . . .'

18

'. . . She's not gonna wake up, son, – she's achieved her life's ambition now . . .'

'. . . y' weren't watchin' Paul Daniels last night, were y', Sep . . .?'

Ten Little Pet Lambs

'Ten little pet lambs
playing in a line
one of them got watery mouth
then there were nine. . . .
Nine little pet lambs
worrying about their mate
one got salmonella
then there were eight. . . .
Eight little pet lambs
heard the engine revvin'
but they never saw the tractor
then there were seven. . . .
Seven little pet lambs
playin' games and tricks
one hanged in wire netting
then there were six. . . .
Six little pet lambs
glad to be alive
tried swimming in the water-trough
then there were five. . . .

Five little pet lambs
bleatin' at the door
the farmer lost his temper
then there were four. . . .
Four little pet lambs
as sweet as you could see
one died of bloody awkwardness
then there were three. . . .
Three little pet lambs
wonderin' what to do
ate a bag of barley meal
then there were two. . . .
Two little pet lambs
the smallest one set-on
to a yow who went and sat on it
then there was one. . . .
One little pet lamb
surprisingly got fat
so we put 'im in the freezer
and that's the end of that. . . .'

'. . . We've got a problem here, Gladys, he's showin' all the signs of being a normal bad-tempered peasant . . .'

'. . . who phoned for you, lads? I was murderin' the auld yow, not the wife . . .'

'. . . so if we count the seven pet lambs, and forget about the five geld gimmers, and if four more yowes drop dead, . . . we'll have a 200 per cent lambin' again . . .'

'. . . it's not worth it, pet, – I'll just have t' put them on again in a couple of hours t' check the lambin' . . .'

Mutton 'Magic'

For a fortnight every year I keep a watchful shepherd's eye on a neighbour's ewes and lambs, while he gently marinates in the Mediterranean.

Having this responsibility for someone else's livestock is an anxious experience. It's far more traumatic than wandering around your own familiar geriatric flock. If one of yours is lying happily dead, that's par for the course, it's no great surprise, and anyway you came to terms with it long ago. But with other people's sheep in your care, – death, disease and disaster are not just fate, or acts of God, or bloody awkwardness, or lack of cobalt, – it's all *your* fault, *you* are entirely responsible.

If some brainless old mule rolls into the well-known missionary position in a rig bottom, you feel *you* should've been there when she did it, to kick her up onto her feet again. If some greedy lamb sticks his head through the pig-netting fence to eat the winter barley in the next field, and hangs himself, – *you* (and only you) should've been waiting nearby to belt him across the nose before he choked to death.

This year I was hoping to get through the whole two weeks without a fatality, and we almost made it. I might have known it was unlikely, a silly naïve expectation, – and sure enough on the penultimate morning this superb lamb was lying very deceased just inside the gate. There had been no warning of trouble, no indication that he might be feeling poorly.

I can only assume that all the sheep in that field, aware that my stewardship was almost at an end, had secretly drawn lots during the night, to decide which one of them would have the privilege of dropping dead for no apparent reason. They were all pretending they knew nothing about it, of course, but I could see the self-satisfied smirks on their faces, – they knew they'd won again.

I've long since come to the conclusion that sheep have an approach to life and death similar to some of those extremist religious sects in the Middle East. You know, – the ones who tend to drive a wagonload of dynamite into a brick wall to impress the opposition. Though to be fair, to give credit where it's due, sheep do seem to have a more highly developed imagination when it comes to thinking up ways to reach that glorious worm-free pasture in the sky.

Of course I'm hardly telling experienced shepherds anything they don't know already. Most of them will have had the big fat yow who manages to get onto her back, with her head downhill, five minutes after she was checked in the morning, so that she has plenty of time to be comfortably expired five minutes before you get round again in the evening. Personally I can't ever remember having a big fat yow, but I do recall several small emaciated ones who performed similar tricks, occasionally even lying across the rig top, which I considered was a bit of unnecessary show-off.

You will all have had your fair share of 'drowners', I expect. Yes, I thought so, – witty young gimmers who totally ignore the clean, galvanised water-trough you provided at great expense, preferring instead to fight their way into a fenced-off ditch for a drink, where they become thoroughly bogged down and die of exhaustion. Meanwhile the lambs, playing with carefree abandon along the dyke back, have managed to fall into the galvanised trough and can't find their way out. They drown as well.

I once had a sick ewe who had been trying unsuccessfully to die for several days. Eventually, thinking perhaps there was a glimmer of hope, I brought her into a loose box for treatment (I was very young and quite inexperienced at the time). I filled her up with every antibiotic wonder drug known to man (or at least everything I could find on the top of the kitchen cupboard with an expiry date after the Second World War), gave her sweet new-mown hay, and delicious ewe and lamb coarse mixture, clean straw on the floor, – everything in fact that might make her feel I cared. There was no water in the building, so I regularly filled up an old pan with fresh, clean water for the old girl. She lasted about forty-eight hours.

You've guessed it, – I found her on the second day lying very comfortably with her nose in the bottom of the pan, drowned in two inches of water. I swear she was smiling.

The history of sheep farming is littered with such tales. Like the new tup who found his way into the grain store the night after we'd paid a fortune for him at Kelso Sales, and quickly consumed about a hundredweight of barley, before he virtually blew up. I expect he arrived at the Pearly Gates stoned out of what might be euphemistically called his 'mind'.

Or the half-bred 'chaser' we once had who insisted on grazing by the roadside rather than in a field of maiden seeds. There by the highway he would occasionally challenge passing traffic to a 'duel'. He only had one real head-to-head confrontation, and he won that (by which I mean he actually came second, – but it would be the ultimate victory for him).

But finally let me tell you of a new 'death trick' for sheep, – at least it's new to me.

I was walking down the main street, minding my own business, when this fellow peasant stopped me. 'I was hoping to see you,' he said eagerly, – 'you being so fascinated by sheep behaviour. I wanted to tell you about a lamb of mine that killed itself last week . . .' He seemed quite excited. Anyway, it appears this bloke had one of those metal hay hecks, you know the sort of thing I mean, – it's a V-shaped wire-meshed container for hay or silage. You slide the lid back, fill it up with a couple of bales, close the lid again, and fasten it down against the wind with a chain that has a hook on the end. The hook goes through a staple on the frame. This particular one was empty, but had been left in the field since winter. Young lambs tend to play and chase each other around objects like this, and one very bright lamb, having licked and nibbled at the chain, had somehow managed to swallow the hook. By the time his devoted shepherd came upon the scene, he was caught fast like a mentally retarded trout.

When old sheep sit around at night chatting about their ancient legends and mythologies, – that lamb will be considered a hero.

'. . . I don't know why we go to parties, – if there's not another farmer there he just doesn't speak to anybody . . .'

'. . . any last requests . . .?'

'. . . don't know about you, Willie, – but we always seem t' be a little bit short of grass at this time of year . . .'

'. . . who said sheep rustlin' was easy money then, – for God's sake let's stick t' robbin' banks from now on . . .'

'. . . I've got to get out of the car park before the heavy mob come lookin' for luck money . . .'

Five Heifers t' the Mart

'The wagon came and peeped the horn
about an hour late
I'd had the heifers organised
since roughly half past eight . . .
the driver he was foamin'
can't repeat just what he said
but the first pick-up he'd had that day
the bloke was still in bed . . .
so he hadn't had his breakfast
just a cup of tea
and still a dozen calls t' make
after he left me . . .
but all the beasts were ready
and the gates all tied wi' twine

they should walk straight up the tailboard
and be gone by half past nine . . .
well four went in no bother
but one refused t' join
and when the driver hit 'er
she just kicked 'im in the groin . . .
that kinda took his breath away
stopped all his dull complainin'
and he stood there bent up double
while the weather started rainin' . . .
we tried again t' get 'er in
twisted tail and swearin'
but she just ran about in rings
wi' goggly eyes a'glarin' . . .
the other four came t' the back
t' look at all the fuss
just as the bitch leaped out the pens
in front of our school bus . . .
off down the road tail in the air
smashed through all the gates
and only stopped when she got back
in amongst her mates . . .
she was surely mad a-bullin'
so there's not much we could do
but that driver won't get randy
for at least a day or two . . .
    he slowly upped the tailboard
    and seemed disinclined t' speak
    I wonder if he'll still come back
    'cos she's got t' go next week . . .!'

'. . . wake up, sleepin' beauty, – you've got visitors . . .'

'. . . and come the peasants' revolt, you'll be the first t' go, brother . . .!'

'. . . alright, alright, you win, – we'll be delighted to extend your overdraft . . .'

'. . . I felt obliged to bring 'im in, Doctor, – it's his wellies, he's not had them off since October 1984 . . .'

'. . . Whoops, sorry, Charlie . . .'

Well I Never

'The old man sighed and scratched his head
can't believe my eyes he said
combines cut two fields a day
silage baled up just like hay
lambing sheds complete with telly
pictures from a gimmer's belly
helicopters up there spraying
tractor cabs with music playing
intervention barley now
quotas for the dairy cow
and who'd believe we'd see the likes
of grown men riding round on trikes . . . ?'

'. . . it's his Lordship, Sep, – he must've heard what y' paid for grass parks yesterday . . .'

'. . . I think y' could be breakin' a few rules here, Willie . . .'

'. . . Dad, what time does Mother get back from the WI . . .?'

'. . . right, that's it, – I want a divorce immediately . . . !'

'Magic' Moments

I often feel that I was never adequately equipped to be a proper peasant. I don't mean physically, – most of the necessary bits and pieces other peasants have are in place, – but temperamentally there's definitely an important virtue missing. Above all, my parents neglected to include enough patience in their combined genes, and I've grown up (more or less) as one of the world's worst waiters.

Once upon a time of course it was assumed in some quarters that all you really needed to be a competent peasant was the rugged physique of a rural Rambo, with hands like fork-lift trucks, enormous feet (probably webbed and smelly), together with the limited imagination of a Cheviot hogg. I doubt if that was ever enough, but perhaps it was more valid yesterday, when life was at walking pace and more predictable, with one-gear horses and permanent pastures. Maybe patience was taken for granted then, a sort of built-in extra, like power steering. However, now that we all run like hell through a maze of quotas, clawbacks, co-responsibility levies and conservationists, in a frenetic scramble to achieve the life-style of a solicitor, – that talent seems more essential than ever. If young son and heir insists upon being a farmer, – he'll have to beg, borrow or steal some patience from somewhere. I would gladly donate a bit of mine, but, as I say, I've never had enough.

Now this wouldn't matter much if I was a 'flying picket', happy to stand about in a Portacabin, reading the *Sun* and hurling occasional abuse at passing policemen. Or a traffic warden, who wanders lonely in a menacing cloud, searching for wayward cars on yellow lines. Or a telephonist, perhaps, in directory enquiries, who although bombarded by flashing lights and ringing bells pleading for her attention, stubbornly finishes varnishing her nails or knitting a balaclava for her burglar boyfriend before taking any notice. Or the council road-mender who spends all day staring into a pothole with an air of cleverly cultivated urgency.

But perhaps I'm confusing patience with apathy. Without a smidgin' of patience the peasant runs the risk of an early cardiac, or at least a hernia, – but he simply can't *afford* apathy. Apathy only allows the mildew to rot his barley before he gets there with the sprayer, or tempts the weather to break when the hay is ready while he's still servicing the baler. Patience, on the other hand, might help him to cut corn at 17 per cent rather than 27 per cent.

That's easy enough to say, but how on earth does a normal, frantic, bad-tempered farmer stand about twiddling his thumbs, waiting calmly for a contractor to arrive with the combine? You *know* it's going to rain just as he drives into the field. You're *sure* another farmer has bribed him to stay where he is and cut another twenty acres. As the sky blackens, the shakewind howls, and everybody round about is into their last field, – the anxiety can be too much.

At the mart I always wanted my livestock sold *now*, convinced the ballot was 'fixed' if I wasn't in the first twenty into the ring. That idle, patient tea-drinking in the canteen was a waste of time. So was all that 'informed' chat while leaning on your pen discussing the trade. Furthermore there was always the added risk that someone might ask what you thought your creatures were worth. That could be very embarrassing. And yet I never abandoned my lot until they were sold. Mind you, as soon as the hammer finally fell, I was off like a lurcher, – anyone seeking luck money had to be very alert indeed.

So what was I in such a frantic rush to get home for? – probably to bale some hay a day too early, or hurriedly clip some sheep with no rise yet, or some such job that would be better left, and done better, with patience.

But it's not easy, – for instance it can be very annoying waiting for a grain wagon. Merchants tend to make an issue about loading times at farms. 'We can't afford to have the vehicle standing in your yard for more than an hour,' they say, – 'time is money, y' know.' So the desperate peasant, who doesn't want any delay either, agrees to load the monster truck at five in the morning, and invests in a mechanical shovel or an auger big enough to empty an intervention store in twenty minutes. Anything to keep the merchant happy, and the ensuing cheque on course.

Next day, having paced up and down the road all morning, awash with coffee, out of fags but not daring to leave the farm in case the wagon sneaks in while he's down at the village, the poor peasant phones the rich merchant at noon. He's out to lunch, of course, and won't be back 'til two. You bang the receiver back and settle down to mince and chips in a bad fettle. And that's when the wagon drives in.

Perhaps it's these everyday exasperations of farming that eat away at patience. Certainly I find it difficult to sit in a queue at the petrol pumps while some grinning woman searches for the self-service nozzle, then for the hole that leads to her petrol tank. To stand outside a cinema for more than three minutes renders the film unsuitable, and lingering in the early hours for a daughter to emerge from a disco can severely threaten our relationship.

Hospital is another place where 'patient patience' can be stretched to terminal limits. 'Hurry up and wait there' seems to be the rule, and because you're feeling lousy and lost you don't complain. 'Quickly, Mr Smith, we've got to get you down to X-ray, we haven't got all day, and they're waiting for you.'

Like hell they're waiting for you. Chances are you'll be left

sitting in the corridor for three days suffering from exposure and malnutrition before your turn comes up.

And what about restaurants? I know a man who, having had dinner at a posh eating house, then had to sit for ages waiting for his bill. He asked repeatedly and politely, but no one took any notice of his eagerness to pay and be off. Eventually he stood up and prepared to leave, at which point half the staff fell upon him waving little bits of paper.

'Your bill, sir,' said the head waiter, smiling the smarmy smile of someone who believes he's just rendered you an immense and personal favour. But this bloke didn't so much as pause as he proceeded to the exit. 'Here's my card,' he said coolly when he reached the door, 'send your bill to the address shown, and in due course it will be paid . . . goodnight.'

I wish I'd done that, but I never had the nerve, or the card.

However, farming remains the ultimate waiting game, you can't hurry it. We can panic ourselves, frantic, foul-mouthed and frustrated, but the weather will change, the corn will ripen, the yowes will lamb, when they're good 'n' ready. As you read this you're probably waiting for the rain to stop (or start), waiting for a mechanic, an electrician, or the postman. Waiting for the wife to bring the car back so you can hurry to the mart, waiting for the phone to ring or the kettle to boil.

Have patience. Didn't your mother tell you, – it'll never boil if you sit and watch it.

'. . . I don't care what you say, Sister, – I cannot accept he was actually *born* like that . . .'

'... come bye t' me, Sweep, – pretend y' haven't seen them ...'

'. . . give 'im time, Sep, – he can still grow up t' be a big fat farmer like yourself, without a hormone implant . . .'

'. . . there's . . . er . . . one less pet lamb t' feed tonight, Gladys . . .'

'. . . sorry, darlin', but I haven't really got the hang of these things yet . . .'

Land of Milk and Money

'He always had a yearning for the simple country life,
away from noisy traffic and the inner city strife, —
farming was a passport to a future more worth while,
where the living had some meaning, bit of freedom, touch of
    style . . .
so when old Jake retired and was looking for a bid,
he took his chance and wrote a cheque for umpteen thousand quid, —
the bank rushed out to help him and drew up a special plan,
eager to accommodate a forward thinking man . . .
repayments were no problem, way ahead the view was clear,
provided he worked night and day for nigh on forty years, —
the Ministry, the EEC, were keen to give him money,
half the world was starving, and here was milk and honey . . .
get your finger out and go like hell, we'll gladly show you how
to get a million gallons from a herd of ninety cows, —
so he borrowed, and invested, and he built up quite a herd,
and milk flowed oh so freely like the spring song from the
    birds . . .
parlour, concrete, slurry pit, silage clamp supreme,
the ideal "mod" foundations for his economic dream, —
it took him twenty years to get the business going right,
just enough to pay the bank, and sleep sometimes at night . . .
he often thought of barley yields and subsidies for yowes,
but the type of farm he'd fashioned now was made for milking
    cows, —

and provided he could raise the herd to maybe ninety-five,
his family and his way of life could somehow just survive . . .
but the postman came and pushed a thing called quota through his
    door,
and suddenly his limit was reduced to sixty-four, —
impossible, ridiculous, he couldn't pay his way,
if he couldn't milk as many cows as he milked yesterday . . .
the bank was sympathetic, and they wept in Lombard Street,
    as they pulled the bloody carpet out from underneath his
    feet. . . .'

'. . . well, y' don't think I'm buyin' another bloody lawnmower, do y' . . .?'

'. . . leave yer Dad alone, – y' know he always feels unwell when the bank statement comes . . .'

'. . . no, Mother, it's not the stuff Henry Cooper advertises, – they're busy with silage this week . . .'

'. . . Shh, put it back, Charlie, – if that bloke Scargill hears about this we'll never get the hole filled in again . . .'

'. . . this is a crisis meeting to agree new quotas on pocket money and a clawback on the housekeeping . . .'

56

The Farm Office

'It's a scene of desolation
as you tiptoe through the door
brown envelopes and crumpled bills
an ashtray on the floor
Burdizzo calf castrator
on the ring-stained window sill
and a cup of last week's coffee
congealed and cold and still
some golf clubs in the corner
and a pair of garden shears
and a can of old Thibenzole

that's been there for umpteen years
and a pocket calculator
that's used to do the VAT
but I left it on last Sunday
and now the battery's flat
the telephone is ringing
from underneath a heap
of circulars and more advice
on management for sheep
the desk's submerged in paper
like a well-used council dump
invoice statement red demand
and a broken water pump
grey filing cab'net bulging
with accounts from long ago
hard black books that tell the tale
of farming's ebb and flow
pencils with no lead inside
pens that never write
rubbish in a cardboard box
that should be set alight
BUT OUT, DON'T TOUCH, DON'T REARRANGE, –
don't tidy up come spring
leave my office well alone
or I'll never find a bloody thing . . . !'

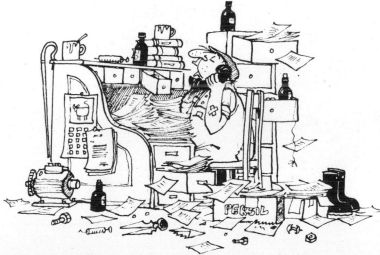

'. . . well, serves 'im right sneakin' up like that . . .'

'. . . I want it back . . .'

'. . . I'm a worried man, Doctor, – it looks like staggers t' me . . .'

'. . . been putting in or taking out, Sep . . .?'

'. . . for God's sake don't switch off, Charlie, – you've only got about thirty seconds t' clip this one . . .'

Nursery Rhyme

'Mary had a little lamb
I'm glad it wasn't mine
cos' its fleece came out in handfuls
and it suffered from the pine . . .
Mary stuffed it full of cobalt
and a dose of copper neat
which didn't cure the shot-jaw
or the rotten scalded feet . . .
it also got pneumonia
and staggers in the spring
it couldn't even run away
the knackered brainless thing . . .
it hung about for ages
and then it broke her heart
when it dropped down dead last Wednesday
in the ring at Hexham Mart. . . .'

'. . . the latest technology, sir, a unique opportunity, sir, immediate delivery, sir, special deferred terms, sir, cuts fifty acres a day, sir, – a glass of wine, sir . . . ?'

'. . . seems the little creep has thirty Swaledale ewes and a cow somewhere north of Darlington . . .'

'. . . there y' are then, lads, – all fixed, off y' go . . .'

Gentlemen v Players

'It's not that they're evil dishonest or wicked
those garlicy foreigners over the sea
but the frogs and the others have never played cricket
so they've not much in common with you sir and me. . . .
They haven't the breeding the style or the touch
for the Englishman's favourite game
I wouldn't of course say they're scoundrels as such
but they never can hope to be quite the same. . . .

Well imagine a Frenchman bowling at Lord's
and probably underhand too
then flogging his onions down by the boards
when third man had nothing much better to do . . .
or the Krauts marching out in Bavarian shorts
to the sound of a noisy brass band
playing Deutschland über alles of course
with a massive great sausage stuck in each hand . . .
and the mafia would run the Italian team
both the umpires suitably bribed
fine leg would be busy selling ice-cream
and we'd find there were fourteen blokes in their side. . . .
Play up play up and keep a straight bat
from April right through to September
you're joking old chap forget about that
they're not British you've got to remember . . .
all those Spaniards the Greeks the Belgians the Dutch
all those plebs from the EEC
good lord it's expecting a little too much
when they don't even stop for afternoon tea. . . !'

'. . . what will we do, Alfie? – the Common Market's going to spoil everything if they make you redundant . . .'

'. . . Gladys, look up that Mutual policy and check if your mother's covered for drownin' . . .'

'. . . all I said was, "here's a cheque for half m' overdraft" . . .'

'. . . good idea, isn't it . . . ?'

Mechanical 'Magic'

I remember one lovely June morning long ago, when I was very young, eager to impress, and not very bright, – leaping out of bed at about 4.30 am to cut some hay. I only did that once.

Undoubtedly the plan was to mow the whole field before breakfast, without a single stop of course, astonishing all my 'lazy' neighbours, – and then, intoxicated by this triumph, go on to dehorn all the calves, worm the lambs and top-dress fifty acres before dinner time. In the afternoon I would dip a few hundred old yowes, have a quick cup of tea (standing up), dig the foundations for a new grain shed, and spend a leisurely evening cleaning out a blocked drain.

Whenever I had silly plans like that (and I don't have them now) the whole schedule would fall apart very early. On that hay-cutting exercise the reaper fell apart at 4.45.

It was one of those old-fashioned red Bamlett mowers, weighing about three tons, driven from massive toe-crushing iron wheels, through an enormous gearbox filled with cogs swimming in oil, to a connecting rod that bent like warm plasticine, which was attached (most of the time) to a knife that quickly became either blunt or toothless, which in turn ran through a row of 'fingers' that were seldom in a straight line, on towards a 'shedder bar' that simply shattered if hit by a thistle.

The thing was a disaster. It was no use going into a field without a trailer-load of spares. Spare blades and rivets for the knife, a hammer, a boxful of spanners, about a year's supply of oil and grease, a spare shedder, a spare con-rod, – another hammer, to replace the first one which would undoubtedly be thrown away after I'd hit my thumb for the third time. A sackful of nuts and bolts and washers was essential to replace all those that would rattle loose, a piece of string, perhaps, if only

to act as a tourniquet to staunch the inevitable flow of blood as you battled with this monster. And one more hammer to replace the second one which would surely fall out of the overloaded tool-box.

Obviously this was way back before the modern breed of mower than can now cut its way through wire at the speed of light. Before progressive peasants moved on to flat-eight systems or big round bales, or abandoned the 'thrills' of haymaking altogether to concentrate on silage, maybe even stuffed into plastic bags. Before 'silent' cabs rattled to the sound of Radio One, and shepherds looked their flocks by trike. With the old Bamlett it took days of continuous trauma to chew your way through a five-acre plot, by which time the headland was 'muck', and the barley ready to harvest anyway.

The first hay turner I had was a converted horse-drawn contraption with weird octopus-like tines that readily came off and hid in the crop until the baler picked them up. The baler didn't like them.

Some years later I acquired what was then the ultimate in hay-making gear, a devilish cunning invention called the Acrobat, – there are still a few about, probably blocking holes in hedges. The great talent of this machine was not turning the hay over, but rather wrapping the whole crop into one endless unbreakable length of green rope, into which the fiercest sun could scarcely penetrate.

Later still we 'progressed' to a wuffler, and there's no doubt this wuffler wuffled splendidly, – no hay was more thoroughly wuffled. The trouble was it would only perform at the pace of an auld yow riddled with footrot and mastitis. Wuffling became a very tedious affair.

I have never actually owned a baler. It could be argued that I always considered them far too expensive (and they undoubtedly are), but to be fair the real reason was my total inability to understand the workings of any piece of machinery more complex than a sack-barrow. Every time I was left in charge of a baler (someone else's of course) even for ten minutes while the other bloke had his coffee break, the damned thing would stop tying knots, or smash a sheer-bolt, or churn out ten-feet bales, or swallow one of those old turner tines.

I wouldn't dare drive a modern combine either, not even from one end of a field to the other, – for sure it would pick up the only available rock on the farm. Elevators would grind to a halt, belts would snap, riddles would block up, lights would flash, and in a state of abject panic I would probably drive into the tractor and trailer leading off. It would be as wise to put me in charge of a space shuttle to the moon.

Of course not everyone will understand this mechanical incompetence. Those who talk constantly and knowledgeably about big ends and cam shafts, and have probably modified their rotary muck spreader to generate cheap electricity, may well feel very superior. Those enthusiasts who like to spend their holidays lying under a warm clutch, or lovingly dismantling their twenty-year-old Escort just so they can clean a plug and put it all together again, may even pity me. But I don't care, – I've come to accept long ago that all my fixed agricultural equipment will sooner or later rattle loose, – that my deadstock will inevitably behave as if it were alive, – teasing at my sanity, grabbing at my skinned knuckles and bruised black thumbnails. Machines just don't like me, and it's mutual.

Over the years the only way I've survived (just) the technological revolution is by resorting to a strategy impressed upon me by my father. When he was the victim of some mechanical disaster, the poor fellow would sadly and silently view the offending beast for perhaps five minutes of statuesque contemplation. Then he would kick it. That would be followed by an impressive tirade of obscene abuse, and then he'd limp back to the house to telephone for a mechanic. It's a technique that's worked pretty well on the whole, but maybe inadvisable if you happen to be wearing wellies at the time.

And that's probably what I don't like about machines, they always get the better of me in the end, – and I'm sure they'd laugh if they could.

'. . . this is ridiculous, Sep, – I've got to pick up Mother sooner or later . . .'

'. . . well, it's got a touch of mildew, a dash of yellow rust, a wee bit of eyespot, – and an auld dead yow . . .'

'. . . I'd better tell y', mister, it's about a week before this stuff takes effect, – then everything just withers away . . .'

'. . . oops, looks like his last sheer bolt's gone as well . . .'

'. . . that's well over her quota, isn't it, Willie . . .?'

Star Quality

'The lady cannot help but please
no animal can beat 'er
milk 'n' butter cream 'n' cheese
and when she's done y' eat 'er . . .
call 'er Gladys Lulu Elsie
She's class out on her own
keep her pregnant fed and healthy
and she'll seldom stray from home . . .
an agricultural glamour girl
with a figure made for just
producin' bottled pure white wine
   from a double-breasted bust. . . .'

'. . . on your marks . . . get set . . .'

'... *what* outstanding account, – you don't expect me to pay for the stuff, do y' ...?'

'. . . and of course everyone tends to have their own individual style . . .'

'. . . C'mon Sep, it's not that bad, – the summer holidays don't *really* last for ever . . .'

'. . . now that's what I call an interestin' lie, Arthur . . .'

Par for the Course

'See him early every morning
when the dew's still on the clover
when the countryside is stretching
when the day is turning over . . .
long before the office opens
and the city stirs awake
long before the phones are answered

and the world is on the make . . .
see him looking stock and counting
with an eye that knows the score
see the canny shepherd wanderin'
like a thousand times before . . .
but today is there a difference
is he staring at the ground
is he standing statuesque and still
with his stick the wrong way round . . .
is he swinging at a thistle
walking on a pace or two
then attacking harmless buttercups
with a vicious follow through . . . ?
the dog looks on bewildered
and the yowes try not to stare
but they know he's got a problem
and he hasn't got a prayer . . .
the poor man's hooked forever
it's the dreaded bug for sure
he's a peasant Ballesteros
and there isn't any cure. . . .
    See him early every morning
    when the dew's still on the car
    when the countryside is dreaming
    and he's seven under par. . . !'

'. . . well, what do y' expect, Missus, he's just a simple country lad, he's never seen anything like this before . . .'

'. . . wake up, y' fool, – this is the third night running you've spent mending the damn combine . . .'

'. . . we only asked him to stop cutting for a couple of days, so that we could save the endangered Bolivian Blue from the jaws of the combine . . .'

'. . . no time t' waste, he says, I'll keep it goin' over dinner time, he says, – nuthin' to it, he says . . .'

Alternative 'Magic'

The trouble with being an umpteenth-generation farmer is that you come to believe you're totally unsuitable for anything else. Of course you may never have *wanted* to do anything else. However, the chances are that having been born, bred and brainwashed into thinking only *real* people shovel slurry, wallow in clarts, cough and wheeze in a cloud of grain dust, spray themselves with obscure chemicals, clean the backsides of sheep, remove the horns and genitals from unfortunate calves, and go about permanently reeking of poor-quality silage, – then no other job would satisfy you now anyway.

And you've got a point I suppose, – well where else could anybody have all that, and the thrill of gambling a fortune every month with the bank manager's money? It's too good to be true, isn't it? Certainly as soon as we could swear and climb into a pair of wellies, our fathers stuffed a stick into one hand, a syringe into the other, and sent us out to do the lambing. That naïve embryo peasant thought it was all his own idea, but it wasn't y' know. That was the time when farming parents depended on their sons to follow the chosen calling, – all other professional avenues were hidden, blocked off, – no other subject was worthy of discussion, – no playmate suitable unless she came from sound agricultural breeding stock, or was filthy rich.

It's not quite as bad as that now of course, youth has a new self-reliance, – a mind of its own that yesterday's generation found harder to cultivate. Anyway, for most of us 'mature beasts' it's far too late to change direction, but I sometimes wonder what else we might have done had we escaped 'the peasant grip'. Well quite a lot I suspect, not necessarily because we were academics, with two 'O' levels, or courted a nubile aristocrat, – but it's arguable that if you can make a living at farming, especially in this climate, – anything's possible!

Well, how about being a schoolteacher for a start? Yes I know most of us are bad-tempered, have little patience, and don't know the difference between the square on the hypotenuse and a Shakespeare sonnet, – but neither do many kids who've been at school for the past fifteen years. Actually they've probably only been at school for about five out of the past fifteen years, – and so have the teachers of course. On that basis I think I could put up with a fair bit of juvenile delinquency and hooliganism, plenty time to recover from it.

However, maybe you don't fancy six or seven weeks holiday in the middle of harvest, and you may even reckon the pay is inadequate. So let's consider a job where money is no object, the kind of lucrative number that ensures we drive a fancy car, and live in a classy detached pad where no one else can afford the rates. You've guessed it, – if you really want to ride the gravy train, get into the legal business. Once you're in they can hardly touch you, because they make the rules for everything. Buying or selling a house, dealing with Granny's will, prosecuting the bloke who ran over your garden gnome, defending the gnome as well.

It's a great job, and you might end up as a Judge.

Still, maybe you don't see yourself in a long black frock and a poncey white wig, and I can understand that, – so what else could we do?

Personally I never fancied being a doctor or a dentist, well rewarded though these professions may be. Well, one of them only meets people who are unwell and miserable, and sneezing, and clutching their bad back, and that can't be much fun, even if all you're required to do is listen to their chests and prescribe antibiotics. And I wouldn't be a dentist for all the grain in the EEC. Spending the working day groping about among rotten molars with a saliva pump must be very boring, – and surely when you've seen the inside of one mouth, you've seen them all.

Anyway, I think I'd want to be out and about in some fresh air. Reading meters for the Water Board looks attractive, no talent required. All you've got to do is lift the manhole cover, read the clock and send the figures to the accounts department, who will multiply them several times before they're dispatched to the astonished customer.

A vet, maybe, sounds pretty straightforward, – inject everything with assorted expensive drugs, and even if the old yow dies (and it probably will) you still get paid. The main problem with being a vet is that it takes half a lifetime to qualify, and then for another twenty years you are the junior partner who does all the Caesareans in the middle of a thirty-acre field on a wet night in February.

I couldn't be a plumber or an electrician. What goes on in the intestines of a telephone or a Hotpoint Automatic is no concern of mine, and beyond my comprehension anyway. A company rep holds no attractions either. At the first sign of apathy, let alone consumer resistance, most farmers turned salesmen would be inclined to say something like 'please yourself, bonny lad', or perhaps an even briefer well-known phrase, and drive off to an early redundancy.

Politics is surely a non-starter. Although we peasants regularly tell lies, we're not really good enough at it for Westminster standards.

Accountancy would be a problem I think, even with a desk full of calculators and an office full of long-legged secretaries. I never *could* understand a balance sheet.

I feel I could have been a vicar, pedalling around the parish being nice to young ladies, and collecting for the organ fund.

And an undertaker may not be a barrel of laughs, but it's probably the 'steadiest' job on earth.

But no, after all this time the job would have to be linked to agriculture in some way, and I think I've hit on the perfect well-paid country situation. It's dead easy, has immense power and influence, and an index-linked pension on retirement. You're right, – a government sheep grader is surely the ultimate job.

Well, just consider what's involved. The man turns up at a couple of marts each week. Somebody wheels in a batch of lambs, a machine weighs them, a clerk works out the half-weight of each animal, and provided (now that the new grading standards apply) the lambs are as lean as a plank of wood, this power-crazed civil servant just knocks off another kilo or so, and dabs them with a spot of paint.

That's it, a run in the country, a leisurely free lunch, no chasing sheep up alley ways or into a wagon, no arithmetic to do, – and home for tea. Anybody can do it, it's a winner. All farmers' sons looking for a way out should apply to the Ministry immediately!

'. . . the straw burning just got a bit out of hand . . .'

'. . . what's your excuse this time, Charlie, – don't tell me you're after her bloomin' lupins . . .?'

'. . . come off it, Sep, – we'll give y' another 50p a ton . . .'

'. . . I think the boss wants t' talk to you, Charlie . . .'

'. . . and just between you 'n' me, Missus, will this machine pull a five-furrow reversible plough on heavy land . . .?'

The Magic Peasant

'I dunno how he does it, –
he always was that way,
and y'd think t' hear 'im talkin'
he never had a lousy day . . .
a chirpy little devil, –
all he touches turns t' gold,
or at least y' might believe so
from the stories that he's told . . .
winter barley would y' credit, –
cut the only sunny week,
yielded four tons t' the acre
as the trade just reached its peak . . .
and the rape was quite outstanding, –
a record yet again,
mind he cut it all one Friday night
before the wind and rain . . .
oh the wheat y'll not believe it, –
nuthin' flat or even bent,
watta crop the biggest ever
all at seventeen per cent . . .
he goes on like this it's painful
it's enough t' make y' cry,
he's got calves that never scitter
he's got yowes that never die . . .
his lambin' is no bother, –
and believe it if you will,

he thinks the grass is greener
on his side of the hill . . .
at the mart the man's a genius, –
trade is slow when he's a buyer,
but bet yer bottom dollar mate
when he's sellin' it's a flyer . . .
he makes hay that's never rained on, –
he's got a hot-line straight t' God,
and I hate the ground he walks on
the clever little sod. . . !'

'. . . where's that new lad gone, Charlie? Tell 'im it's tea time . . .'

'. . . the electricity's gone off, Sep, – and y' know that VAT man y' were expectin'. . .'

'. . . and when brother Walter moves among you, verily those who boldly claimed four tons an acre can surely give more generously . . .'

'. . . only fools and horses out on a morning like this, what . . .'

'. . . it's His Lordship and Lady Daphne, isn't it, Willie? This could mean a massive rent
reduction if we play our cards right . . .'

Tally Ho Ho Ho!

'Polished boots
and scarlet coats
britches cream and tight
hard black hats
and white cravats, –
noisy technicolor sight . . .
shining saddle
whips in hand
whisky flasks galore
platted tails
and ladies' veils, –
the strangest sport you ever saw . . .
stand for ages
in the rain
chilled right to the bone
out of mind
with cold behind, –
perhaps we should've stayed at home . . .
but see the hounds
and hear the horn
pounding big flat feet
the fox has wheeled
across that field, –
through some poor bugger's winter wheat . . .
so plunge the clarts
it's full flight now

jump that if you dare
the dog's on scent
and quite hell bent, –
right on the track of some old hare . . .
then home for tea
with knackered horse
feet and fingers numb
can't quite forget
your bum is wet . . .
    and some folks seem to think it's fun. . . !'

'. . . but y' gotta be jokin', Vicar . . .!'

'. . . what we have here, Rupert, is a serious breakdown in communications . . .'

'. . . alright, George, I'm prepared to accept that your father always sets the tups away on the 21st, – however, the date does have a deeper historical significance as well . . .'

'. . . just another crazy peasant, Sarge, mumbling something about milk quotas and Michael Jopling . . .'

'. . . not on yer life, Sonny, – if you imagine I'm wandering about all winter covered in blue paint
you must be quite mad . . .!'

Poor Auld Dog

'Poor auld Sweep I fear is past it
he's gettin' slow and rather old
and only when the spirit moves 'im
will the dog do what he's told . . .
he's gone grey around the muzzle
and bleary eyes are growing dim
and I've seen him start to limp a bit
when the pressure gets t' him . . .

he's no longer fast and fearless
(if that ever was in fact the case)
and sometimes resignation
clouds his weary hang-dog face . . .
then of course y' must remember
he's got a cauliflower ear
though I sometimes think he's only deaf
when he doesn't want to hear . . .
he's a dog that's had his day perhaps
now he's maybe had enough
and if y' swear and curse at 'im
well he'll quickly take the huff . . .
is he awkward is he lazy?
has he learned a few new tricks?
no he just needs more encouragement
to do the jobs he picks . . .
aye y' gotta make allowances
Sweep's not what he used t' be
and when I come t' think of it
the same applies t' me. . . .'

'. . . no need t' hang about, Willie, – I'm just clearin' the odd blocked drain, that's all . . .'

'. . . any chance of a nice plump bird at about 75p per pound if I come back after dark . . .?'

'. . . I would've thought that was a bit excessive for one reject, wouldn't you, Willie . . .?'

'. . . Well, you've huffed 'er, haven't y', – she reckoned a highly commended was in order at least . . .'

Black and White 'Magic'

My cattle career began with a mixed posse of geriatric cows, who in those early pioneer springs would duly give birth to a miscellaneous collection of multi-coloured calves, more often than not with the calculated boredom of old tarts who'd seen it all before, – and they had, of course, about a dozen times before I got them. They were an ugly bunch, and if ever we topped up the herd with the occasional nubile heifer, old Angus rent-a-bull would go positively silly, and you could hardly blame 'im.

The Queen of this harem, the leader of the pack if you like, was Bridget (probably named after Bardot, but bearing little resemblance to that delectable creature). Our Bridget was a little cross Galloway lady, all hair and belly and big floppy lugs, and after she'd bullied her way through far more than her fair share of feed, she liked nothing better than to wander lazily down to the river for a dip. There she would drink and wallow for a while, before rejoining her companions in her own good time.

One night, however, she got into difficulties after a bit of a flood, and was forced to stumble downstream for about two hundred yards with me in pursuit shouting encouragement from the bank. She eventually managed to scramble out at the ford, just as old Charlie Oswald, an alcoholic chiropodist who lived on the other side of the river, was hiccuping his way merrily across, without a care in the world. Bridget emerged shakily from the turbulent waters, looking (to me at least) like a massive soggy spaniel, but to Charlie, in his condition, as a black hairy monster from the deep. The bewildered man stood there transfixed, up to his knees in water, as Bridget came up, shook herself, gave a snort or two to remove the flotsam from her nose, and waddled off up to the hill back home. They reckon Charlie stayed off the booze for nearly a week.

The main problem with suckler cows, however, is that they eat like walking incinerators. Feeding that lot on a winter's morning could be a hazardous operation, – if you didn't get the feed out of the trailer and yourself out of the field in about three minutes flat, they'd have y' – wellies and all, along with the tractor seat and most of the wiring.

Sooner or later they take over your life, and your land. Through spring and summer all of the farm not actually occupied by these eating machines is devoted to growing fodder for their bottomless bellies, and all winter spent stuffing them with whatever you've grown. Not surprisingly, perhaps, we eventually turned to rearing Friesian calves.

The little twelve-week-old black-and-white bulls were generally bought from a succession of devious dealers from the dark side of the earth beyond Consett. These men were fully paid members of an exclusive nomadic mafia, who roamed from mart to mart buying up one or two calves, until they had a more or less level batch, to sell on to unsuspecting peasants like me.

Not that they were by any means trouble free. There would always be at least one who seemed disinclined to prosper like his mates. This fellow would eat as much as any other calf of course, but instead of converting all that expensive high-protein feed into bone and meat, reasonably distributed over the whole frame, his intake would produce only belly, – an ever-expanding belly at that.

This 'inflating Friesian' would then develop an interesting pattern of ringworm, a cough like a fifty-fags-a-day grandad, and a bowel movement more usually associated with a diet of prunes. Within a matter of weeks he would go on to pick up every obscure bug known to veterinary science, and be transformed from a sleek-skinned young bull, aglow with promises of sirloin and fillet, into a wheezing little spotty pot-bellied wreck, looking more and more like an ageing pregnant dalmation.

However, with loving care, dedicated management, and a bit of luck, the majority would grow on, gaining weight (while losing horns and masculinity), until such time as they went out to grass.

Turning a batch of calves, who've spent all their formative months inside a hemmel, out to grass, can be an interesting exercise. For a start they may well be reluctant to emerge from their hemmel at all. As far as they can ascertain the big nasty world outside is filled with mad farmers wielding sticks, barking, biting dogs and growling machinery. Only a very brave calf would venture into such an unfamiliar world. (On the other hand if by some chance you accidentally fail to secure the gate with barbed wire and padlocks one night before you go to bed, – the whole damn lot will be out in a trice, and half-way to Brighton before dawn.)

Yet after a lot of violent persuasion, cursing, tempting and arm waving, one beast will eventually make the giant leap, unable to contain his bovine curiosity any longer. You might imagine that once this has happened the rest will automatically follow, rather like sheep, – well, they will, all except one, that is, who now finds himself alone in the deserted hemmel, and panics. It could take a posse of peasants the rest of the day to manhandle this poor deranged creature out through the wide-open twelve-foot gate, into the fresh air.

Across the yard and along the road they'll tiptoe as if on hot cinders, wide-eyed and nervous, but the green, clean, delicious field is waiting just around the corner.

Again you might imagine that young calves would take one sniff of new grass, and immediately put their heads down and eat for evermore, 'eyes down for a full bite'. Not these lads, – suddenly free in twenty acres, they take off, round and round the field in a mad, galloping, kicking stampede, until coughing and spluttering and totally exhausted they finally collapse in a heap.

Later they'll find the water-trough, and a taste for the menu. That 'pregnant dalmation' will cough more enthusiastically than ever, a couple will blow up with grassy gasses, several will become lame, one (who you subsequently discover to be inadequately castrated) goes off courting among your neighbour's heifers, another leaps onto the road and is chased for several miles by a long queue of Sunday drivers, and yet another has to be brought back inside after swallowing a Coke tin thrown over the hedge by a passing motorist. That's called summer grazing. Comes the 'back-end' and it's time for the mart, time for a return on these growing investments.

Marting is divided into two philosophies. There are those who believe the ritual to be an essential part of any peasant's lifestyle, a sort of twice-weekly (at least) stimulant taken to sharpen the wits, look into the inadequacies of other people's husbandry, pick up a bargain and some luck money, sell at a profit. These farmers look upon the mart as the perfect market place, where the quick entrepreneur can prosper, and the slow can miss the boat. A stock market with real stock.

Others view the whole exercise as an anachronism and far too risky. They claim it's boring, they have better things to do at home – but that's not entirely true. They seldom venture to the ringside, preferring to buy and sell through groups or co-operatives. On the rare occasions they *do* visit, they look out of place, too well dressed, uncomfortable, anxious, and invariably pay over the odds for broken-mouthed mules with a lamb and a half, – and go home even more convinced the place is a trap organised by a crooked auctioneer for the benefit of devious auld peasants . . . and they could be right.

Certainly there are risks. Will the wagon turn up on time? Will the cattle be ready to load? Will you miss your turn on the ballot? Will the trade be fast or slow? Will that big fat dealer from Yorkshire be there, the one who buys big plain bullocks? Do you know what they're worth? Do you know what you need?

You may end up selling nowt, and buying twenty more. It's a gamble filled with black and white magic.

Meanwhile back at home that 'pregnant dalmation' (you didn't dare take *him* to the mart) is still wheezing expensively.

'. . . dammit, Rupert, countryside's goin' t' the dogs, soon be no decent farming to gallop over . . .'

'. . . gentlemen, you're not concentrating, these sheep are for nothing . . . !'

'. . . it's no fun being a sheep, we're only expected t' get randy once a year, – and in *November* . . .!'

'. . . I just came in to tell 'im I'd bought another farm . . .'

'. . . y' haven't seen Granny anywhere, have you, Sep . . .?'

Son 'n' Heir

'Willie noticed father's temper
at a very early age
saw the veins and colour rising
when he flew into a rage
heard him roaring loud and swearing
full of fire in his belly
or sitting still for hours
staring blankly at the telly
heard him screaming at the telephone
saw him kicking collie dogs
skinning knuckles fingers knees
on spanners chains and cogs
saw him crawling out at midnight
to calve a suckler cow
and getting up at four again
to lamb an old mule yow
saw him coming back in filthy
smelling like a drain
muckin' out the byre
pulling turnips in the rain
saw him take a nasty turn or two
for one thing or another

splutter cough and wheeze a lot
and hardly speak t' Mother . . .
     and yet young little Willie
     who's a normal canny lad
     just can't wait to be a peasant
     like his old demented Dad. . . .'

'. . . this the first time y've brought the missus up for Smithfield, Guv'nor . . .?'

'. . . what's the matter, boys, – had a poor harvest this year . . .?'

'. . . no luck today, gentlemen, – might as well get orf home . . .'

'. . . oh, we can get y' out alright, yer Lordship, – but maybe we should discuss the rent first . . .'

'. . . I wouldn't if I was you, Tommy, – I'm not sure he's in the right frame of mind for it . . .'

126

Right Next to the Road

'If a field of barley turns grey in July
instead of a bright burnished gold
and it's firmly determined to gradually die
you can bet your sweet life it's right next to the road . . .
all disease and disaster and terminal blight
all the tales you don't want to be told
never happen some place far away out of sight
but where everyone sees them right next to the road . . .
the yow that's been missing where the hell can she be
lame and incredibly old
she'll be standing there coughing and wheezing you'll see
in full view of the traffic right next to the road . . .
total strangers from town will drive up to your door
with a chorusing family load
who can't wait to tell you the terrible score
of the cows in the cornfield right next to the road . . .

everything nasty expensive and bad
all the tragedies gently unfold
where your neighbours can see what a cock-up you've had
in that field full of thistles right next to the road. . . .'

'. . . nearly ready, folks . . .'